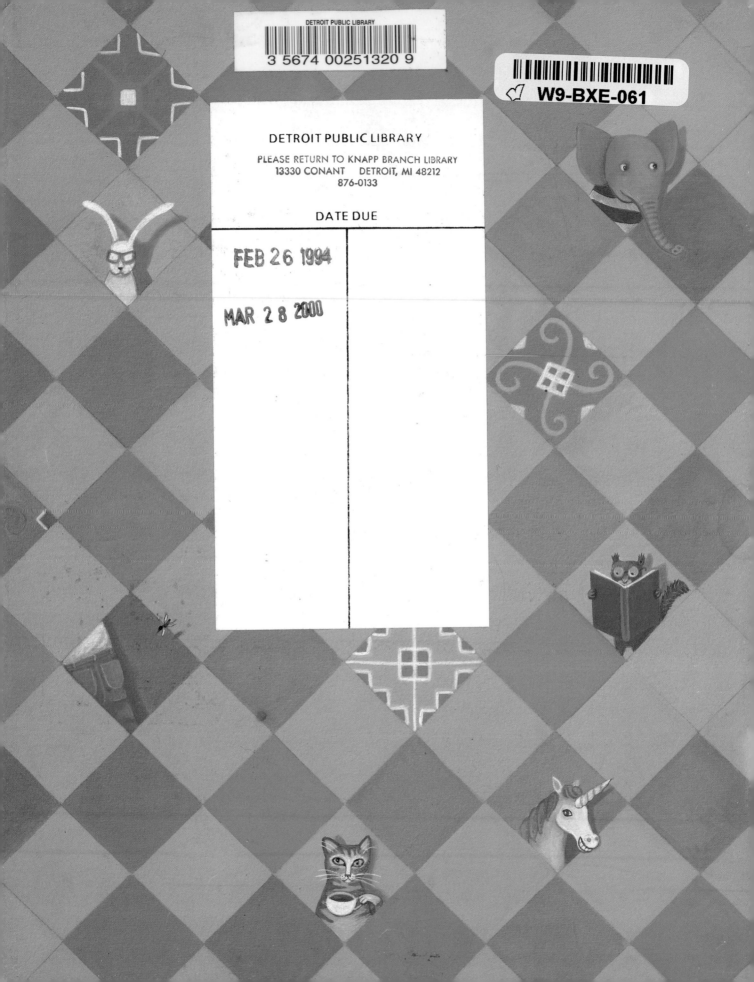

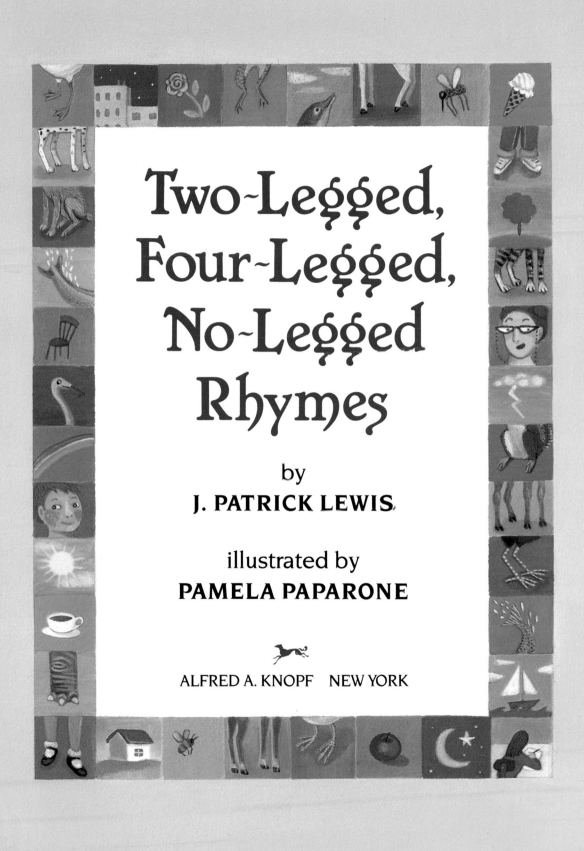

Two-Legged, Four-Legged, No-Legged Rhymes

by

J. PATRICK LEWIS

illustrated by

PAMELA PAPARONE

ALFRED A. KNOPF   NEW YORK

To Myra Cohn Livingston and
Anne Schwartz, without whom . . .
—J.P.L.

To my family
—P.P.

THANKS

Myra Cohn Livingston,
editor of *Dog Poems* (Holiday House, 1990), who first published "Stories"

Paul Janeczko,
editor of *The Places My Words Are Looking For* (Bradbury, 1990), who first
published "Mosquito"

Lee Bennett Hopkins,
editor of *Flit, Flutter, Fly* (Doubleday, 1991), who first accepted "Fireflies"

This is a Borzoi Book published by Alfred A. Knopf, Inc.

Text copyright © 1991 by J. Patrick Lewis
Illustrations copyright © 1991 by Pamela Paparone
All rights reserved under International and Pan-American Copyright Conven-
tions. Published in the United States by Alfred A. Knopf, Inc., New York, and
simultaneously in Canada by Random House of Canada Limited, Toronto.
Distributed by Random House, Inc., New York.

Manufactured in Singapore
Book design by Mina Greenstein
2   4   6   8   10   9   7   5   3   1

Library of Congress Cataloging-in-Publication Data
Lewis, J. Patrick.
Two-legged, four-legged, no-legged rhymes / by J. Patrick Lewis ; illustrated
by Pamela Paparone.   p.   cm. Summary: A collection of poems about such
colorful animals as the porcu-pain, the hippopot, and Paula Koala.
ISBN 0-679-80771-3 (trade)   ISBN 0-679-90771-8 (lib. bdg.)
1. Children's poetry, American. [1. Animals—Poetry. 2. American poetry.]
I. Paparone, Pamela, ill.   II. Title.   PS3562.E9465T9   1991
811'.54—dc20   90-20651   CIP   AC

CONTENTS

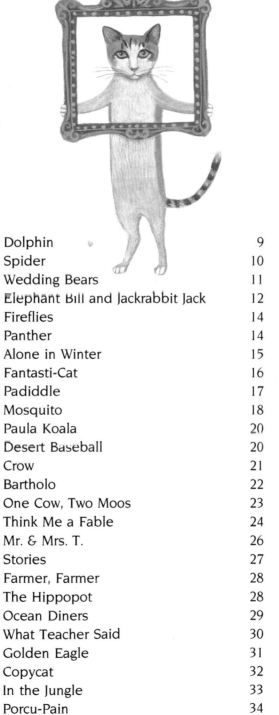

DOLPHIN

If you want to be a snail   hug the shore

If you want to be a bird   skim the sea

If you want to be a whale   plow the wave

If you want to see the world   f o l l o w   m e

SPIDER

Now that she has knit-and-purled
White lace curtains on the world,
She sits patiently all curled.

Something creepy this way crawls
Blindly up the basement walls;
Time to take her curtain calls.

WEDDING BEARS

A panda by the name of Ling-
Ling met another panda, Ping.
They fell in love the first of spring
And hand in hand Ling-Ling and Ping
Planned a panda wedding-ding.
A fling,
A ring,
A wedding-ding!
The sun was shining,
So was Ling-
Ling standing
Hand in hand with Ping.

ELEPHANT BILL AND JACKRABBIT JACK

Did you ever hear about Elephant Bill?
He tramped Elephant grass on Elephant Hill,
He had Elephant ears and an Elephant nose,
And Elephant wrinkles in his Elephant clothes.

Early one morning with the sun on his back,
Old Elephant Bill met Jackrabbit Jack,
Who had Jackrabbit fur and Jackrabbit teeth,
And Jackrabbit jumpers tucked underneath.

Said Jackrabbit Jack to Elephant Bill,
"Let's race to the bottom of Elephant Hill,
Then race back up so that people can see
The mountain that ought to be named after me!"

Elephant Bill gave an Elephant laugh,
He beat Jack downhill by a mile and a half!
But they got to the bottom and had just turned around
When Elephant Bill heard a terrible sound—

The sound that an Elephant never forgets,
Jackrabbit had turned on his back-jumper jets!
And huffing below, old Elephant Bill
Looked up to the top of . . . Jackrabbit Hill.

13

FIREFLIES

An August night—
    The wind not quite
A wind, the sky
    Not just a sky—
And everywhere
    The speckled air
Of summer stars
    Alive in jars

PANTHER

I am as black as coal is black.
And where I go the night steps back.
And where I've been I leave my mark:
Two diamonds flashing in the dark.

ALONE IN WINTER

Have you come upon a doe,
   alone in winter?
I did once. She was shy.
Wind galloped through the trees
And the trees stepped back
And the doe made a slow
circle in the air
with her wet black nose,
as if to say,
I have come upon a boy,
   alone in winter.

FANTASTI-CAT

Mookie James
Fantasti-Cat
Sleeps with an eye
On the thermostat
Keeps it chilly
When it's hot
Turns it toasty
When it's not
Serves the lady
Of the house
Crackers, cheese
& chocolate mouse
Pours her a cup
Of sugar-lump tea
Keeps her purr-
Fect company
Sings her a ditty
Reads her a rhyme
Tickles her toes
From time to time
After midnight
Shadows fly
Lady calls
Her private eye
Mookie James
Fantasti-Cat
Half-asleep
By the thermostat.

16

PADIDDLE

"They must be here *some*where,"
　Said Mrs. McPotts,
Whose dizzy Dalmatian
　Was missing his spots.

"You *had* them at breakfast,
　You wore them outside!
Now, where could one hundred
　And twenty spots hide?"

She ransacked the attic,
　She rummaged through drawers,
She ripped the linoleum
　Tile from the floors!

"Padiddle!" she shouted
　(for that was his name),
"I've never played such
　A ridiculous game!"

And that's when it happened,
　Poor Mrs. McPotts
Snuck a peek in the mirror—
　At Mrs. McSpotts!

MOSQUITO

I was climbing up the sliding board
When suddenly I felt
A Mosquito bite my bottom
And it raised a big red welt.
So I said to that Mosquito,
"I'm sure you wouldn't mind
If I took a pair of tweezers
And I tweezered *your* behind."

He shriveled up his body,
He shuffled to his feet.
He said, "I'm awfully sorry
But a fellow's got to eat!
Still, there *are* Mosquito manners,
And I must have just forgot 'em.
I swear I'll never never *never*
Bite another bottom."

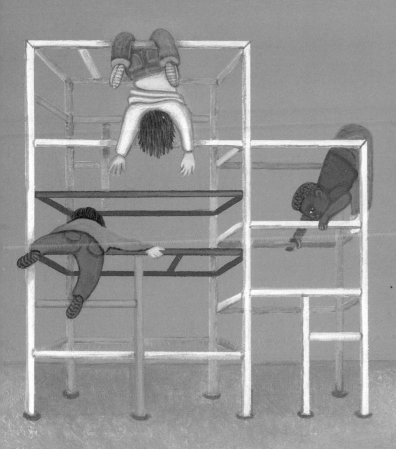

But a minute later Archie Hill
And Buck and Theo Brown
Were horsing on the monkey bars,
Hanging upside down.
They must have looked delicious
From a skeeter's point of view
'Cause he bit 'em on the bottoms—
Archie, Buck, and Theo, too!

You could hear 'em going "Holy✳&!#"
  You could hear 'em going *whack!*
    You could hear 'em cuss and holler,
      Going *smack-smack-smack!*

A Mosquito's awful sneaky,
A Mosquito's mighty sly,
But I never never *never*
Thought a skeeter'd tell a lie!

PAULA KOALA

Paula Koala, the Queen of the Breeze,
Paula Koala, all knuckles and knees,
    Climbs on her tummy
    Like Daddy and Mummy
And sticks to the gummy gum trees.

DESERT BASEBALL

Lizard outfielders
at gnatting practice stretching
to catch a few flies

20

CROW

Jump-Johnny Peacoat
From the day he was born
Pick-pick-picka-pick-
Pecked at the corn.

Jump-Johnny Peacoat
In the winter gone dead
Pulled his collar up
Over his head.

Jump-Johnny Peacoat
In the summer gone light
Sailed tall sunflower
Ships in the night.

BARTHOLO

I love to see
Bartholo jump
And pull the shoestrings
From a shoe.

I love to feel
Bartholo rub
His whiskers next
To me. Do you?

But most of all
I love to hear
Bartholomew.

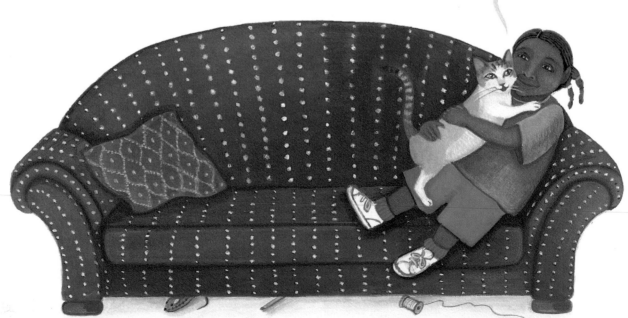

M-E-W!

22

ONE COW, TWO MOOS

We used to have a   single cow,
We called her   Mrs. Rupple.
But she got struck   by a lightning bolt
And now we have a   couple.

She's walking sort   of funny now,
Oh, pity her   poor calf!
Old Mrs. Rupple   gives no milk,
She gives us   half-and-half.

23

THINK ME A FABLE

Lend me an ear, said Mosquito.
Think me a fable, said Fox.
Sleep me good night, said Cricket.
   Crooked field, said Ox.

Slither me home, said Lizard.
Cross me the river, said Moose.
Dance me in circles, said Lobster.
   Fair wind, said Goose.

Crowd me a city, said Pigeon.
Still me a pond, said Frog.
Lift me blue skies, said Eagle.
    Raw bone, said Dog.

Race me the wind, said Cheetah.
Sound me a cave, said Bat.
Leap me the land, said Leopard.
    Top cream, said Cat.

MR. & MRS. T.

Mr. & Mrs. Rainbow Trout,
A spiky, speckled pair,
Wanted to take a trip downstream—
It didn't matter where.

Said Mrs. T. to Mr. T.,
"Let's find ourselves a brook,
A country creek less traveled by"—
And that's the one they took.

Said Mr. T. to Mrs. T.,
"I haven't had such fun
Since somersaulting up the falls
With Rainbows on the run!"

Said Mrs. T., "We've never been
In waters quite so blue.
I'd love to stay the livelong day
Splash-dancing here with you!"

STORIES

Circling by the fire,
My dog, my rough champion,
Coaxes winter out of her fur.
She hears old stories
Leaping in the flames:
The hissing names of cats,
Neighbors' dogs snapping
Like these gone logs,
The cracking of ice . . .
Once, romping through the park,
We dared the creaking pond.
It took the dare and half
Of me into the dark below.
She never let go.

We watch orange tongues
Wagging in the fire
Hush to blue whispers.
Her tail buffs my shoe.
She has one winter left,
Maybe two.

FARMER, FARMER

Farmer Howe milked the cow,
  Missed the bucket,
    Hit the plow.

Farmer Mull milked the bull...
  Wave good-bye
    To Farmer Mull.

THE HIPPOPOT

  The Hippopot-
  amus does not
  come out of wat-
    er holes a lot.
  He finds a bot-
  tom squishy spot
    for his aquat-
    ic Hippo squat.

28

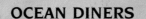

OCEAN DINERS

They open up their beaks and throats
For breakfast off the backs of boats.

Some take a dip and dive for brunch,
Some join the passengers for lunch—

Or swoop in low for sneak attacks
On things like peanut butter snacks.

And when they're in a *hungry* mood,
Sea gulls love your finger food!

WHAT TEACHER SAID

"The Unicorn?"
    said Mrs. Whist.
"The Unicorn
    does not exist.
The horse was never
    born," she said,
"Who wore a horn
    upon his head.
Oh, biffle-bat,
    you silly child,
Such animals
    do not run wild.
I've never seen
    one anywhere!

"…Except for *that*
    one! *OVER THERE!*"

GOLDEN EAGLE

In ruffled coat and ragged pants
He gives the world a wicked glance,

Then lifts himself into the sky,
Now the dashing private eye.

The newborn fawn beyond the trees
Wobbles back on wooden knees.

One leap, and suddenly she's gone!
The golden bird drifts up . . . and on.

COPYCAT

Tom's crazy cat
Played a weird game—
If someone said, "Tom!"
The cat always came.
When Tom drank his milk,
The cat sipped its cream.
If Tom took a nap,
The cat had a dream.
If Tom took a bath,
The cat licked its paw.

I said to *my* cat,
"Why, I never saw
Anything half
As funny as that!"

"Neither did I,"
Chuckled my cat.

IN THE JUNGLE

Snake spells letters, sleepy *O*'s,
S on winding *S*, and goes

Up to see the chimpanzees'
Fingertips connect the trees.

Banana leaves uncurl and blue
Caterpillars drink the dew.

Beneath the big-top tent a pair
Of parrots scold the shadows where

Still and shady creatures hide—
Waiting . . . watching . . . wild-eyed.

PORCU-PAIN

One day, beside a cactus patch,
   I asked a Porcupine
How come he'd poked so many needles
   Up and down his spine.
"Actually," said Porky P.,
   "They aren't really mine.

"A century or so ago
   There was this giant Bee
Whose stinger stung a cousin
   Of my early family.
The stingers went and multiplied,
   And now they're stuck on me!"

I shivered once and quivered twice,
   My voice began to crack.
"How painful it must be for you
   When someone takes a whack!"
"It never hurts," he said, "unless
   I'm sleeping on my back."

THE LION-

He's smarter than the Tabby-
he's braver than the Tom-
he's quicker than the Alley-
he's as big as big cats come.

The Lion is the smartest, bravest, quickest cat
unless
you happen to include his friend, the lovely Lion-
ess.

RED AND GRAY
IN CITY PARK

Gray squirrel, red squirrel
Just about dawn
Peeking from a tree trunk
With their winter coats on.

Come out, red squirrel;
Come out, gray.
Snowy winter's left us
A knee-high day.

Red squirrel, gray squirrel
Just before dark
Sitting on my snowman
Standing in the park.

Come down, gray squirrel;
Come down, red.
I'll give you an acorn
Before I go to bed.

37